Cold Drinks

Ann Redmayne

Illustrated by

Kareen Taylerson

Evans

Dad is running in a marathon today.
We're making cold drinks for the end of the race.

These are the drinks that we'll make.
Banana Milkshake
Strawberry Crush
Celebration Chocolate
Orange Cloud
Grapefruit Honey Milkshake
Fizzy Fruit
Pool

The first thing we must do is wash our hands.

You should always wash your hands and clean all work surfaces thoroughly before preparing food.

BANANA MILKSHAKE

Ingredients

4 bananas
1 litre of milk
4 tsp of soft brown sugar

Utensils

fork
bowl
measuring jug
spoon
liquidizer or
balloon whisk
serving jug

Makes enough for one jug.

I'm mashing the banana.
I'm stirring the milk and sugar together.
Then I will mix everything together in the liquidizer.

Always get an adult to use a liquidizer for you. The blades inside are very sharp.

Most of the drinks in this book should be put in the fridge for two to three hours to cool.

STRAWBERRY CRUSH

Ingredients

200 g of strawberries
1 litre of milk

Utensils

colander
fork
bowl
kitchen knife
chopping board
measuring jug
liquidizer or
balloon whisk
serving jug

Makes enough for one jug.

I like picking strawberries.
You should only pick the soft, juicy, red ones.

If you don't have strawberries in the garden, you can buy fresh or frozen strawberries to use in this recipe.

Whisk or liquidize the milk and strawberries together. Pour into the serving jug and add the strawberry slices.

CELEBRATION CHOCOLATE

Ingredients

4 tbsp of chocolate ice cream
1 litre of milk
Chocolate to grate on the top

Utensils

tablespoon
measuring jug
grater
small plate
4 glasses
spoon

Makes enough for four glasses.

Scooping frozen ice cream from a container is easier if you wet the spoon first.

I've grated the chocolate for you.
Now I can sprinkle it on top of the drinks.

Graters are very sharp. Always get an adult to grate food for you.

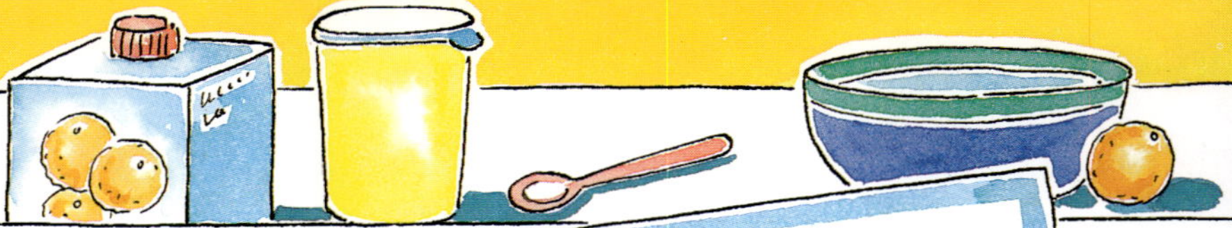

ORANGE CLOUD

Ingredients

1 litre of orange juice
450 g natural yoghurt
1 orange to slice

Utensils

balloon whisk
kitchen knife
serving jug

Makes enough for one jug.

Yoghurt gives the Orange Cloud a nice, creamy taste. You can decorate the drink with slices of orange.

GRAPEFRUIT HONEY MILKSHAKE

Ingredients

500 ml of chilled milk
500 ml of grapefruit juice
2 tbsp clear honey

Utensils

measuring jug
tablespoon
liquidizer or balloon whisk
serving jug

Makes enough for one large jug.

Yoghurt gives the Orange Cloud a nice, creamy taste. You can decorate the drink with slices of orange.

GRAPEFRUIT HONEY MILKSHAKE

Ingredients

- 500 ml of chilled milk
- 500 ml of grapefruit juice
- 2 tbsp clear honey

Utensils

- measuring jug
- tablespoon
- liquidizer or balloon whisk
- serving jug

Makes enough for one large jug.

After she's stirred the honey into the juice, can I add the milk?
Yes, then I will liquidize it for you.

FIZZY FRUIT POOL

Ingredients

600 ml of grapefruit juice
600 ml of apple juice
600 ml of orange juice
600 ml of soda water or fizzy mineral water
Slices of strawberry, banana and cucumber

Utensils

measuring jug
large punchbowl or similar bowl
ladle
12 glasses

Makes enough for 12 glasses.

This recipe is Dad's favourite.
Mixing the fruit juices and fizzy water together is easy.

Now you can float the fruit and cucumber in the bowl.

You should make the Fizzy Fruit Pool just before you are going to drink it so that it doesn't lose its fizz.

To make the drinks really cool, add ice cubes to them just before serving.

And Dad is winning!

Can you remember the names of the drinks that the family prepared for the end of the marathon race? The answers are at the bottom of the page, but don't peep until you have tried yourself.

1. Banana Milkshake 2. Strawberry Crush 3. Celebration Chocolate 4. Orange Cloud
5. Grapefruit Honey Milkshake 6. Fizzy Fruit Pool